This book belongs to:

____

The Alphabet

TRACE THEN WRITE ON YOUR OWN.

TRACE THEN WRITE ON YOUR OWN.

TRACE THEN WRITE ON YOUR OWN.

TRACE THEN WRITE ON YOUR OWN.

TRACE THEN WRITE ON YOUR OWN.

TRACE THEN WRITE ON YOUR OWN.

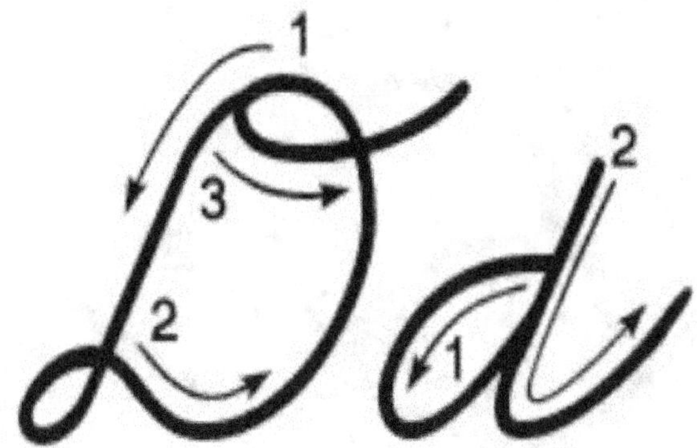

TRACE THEN WRITE ON YOUR OWN.

d   d   d   d   d   d

d   d   d   d   d   d

d

TRACE THEN WRITE ON YOUR OWN.

D   D   D   D   D

D   D   D   D   D

D

d

D

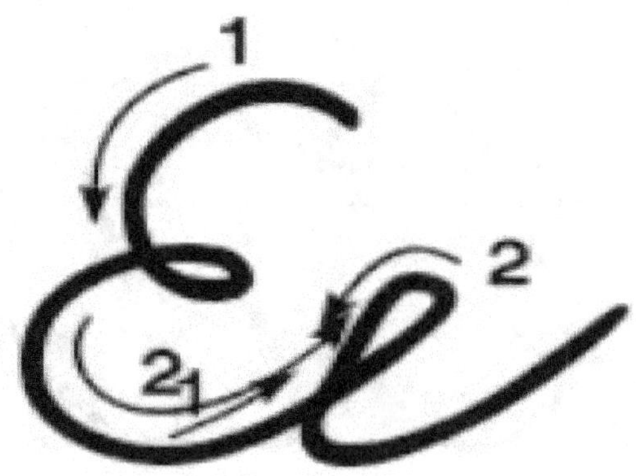

TRACE THEN WRITE ON YOUR OWN.

TRACE THEN WRITE ON YOUR OWN.

TRACE THEN WRITE ON YOUR OWN.

TRACE THEN WRITE ON YOUR OWN.

TRACE THEN WRITE ON YOUR OWN.

TRACE THEN WRITE ON YOUR OWN.

TRACE THEN WRITE ON YOUR OWN.

TRACE THEN WRITE ON YOUR OWN.

TRACE THEN WRITE ON YOUR OWN.

TRACE THEN WRITE ON YOUR OWN.

TRACE THEN WRITE ON YOUR OWN.

j   j   j   j   j
j   j   j   j   j

j

TRACE THEN WRITE ON YOUR OWN.

J   J   J
J   J   J

J

j

J

TRACE THEN WRITE ON YOUR OWN.

TRACE THEN WRITE ON YOUR OWN.

TRACE THEN WRITE ON YOUR OWN.

TRACE THEN WRITE ON YOUR OWN.

TRACE THEN WRITE ON YOUR OWN.

TRACE THEN WRITE ON YOUR OWN.

TRACE THEN WRITE ON YOUR OWN.

TRACE THEN WRITE ON YOUR OWN.

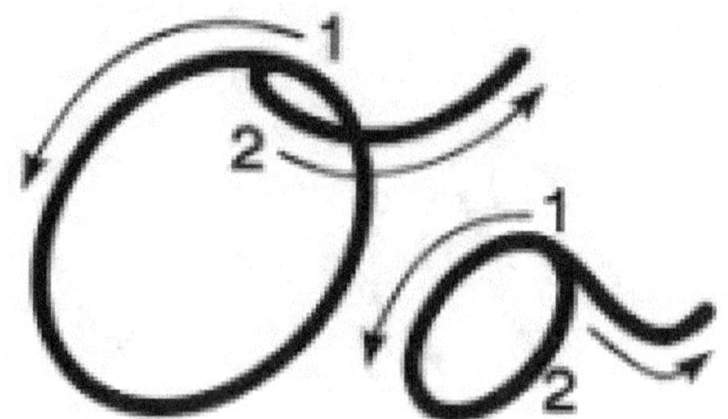

TRACE THEN WRITE ON YOUR OWN.

TRACE THEN WRITE ON YOUR OWN.

TRACE THEN WRITE ON YOUR OWN.

TRACE THEN WRITE ON YOUR OWN.

TRACE THEN WRITE ON YOUR OWN.

TRACE THEN WRITE ON YOUR OWN.

TRACE THEN WRITE ON YOUR OWN.

TRACE THEN WRITE ON YOUR OWN.

TRACE THEN WRITE ON YOUR OWN.

TRACE THEN WRITE ON YOUR OWN.

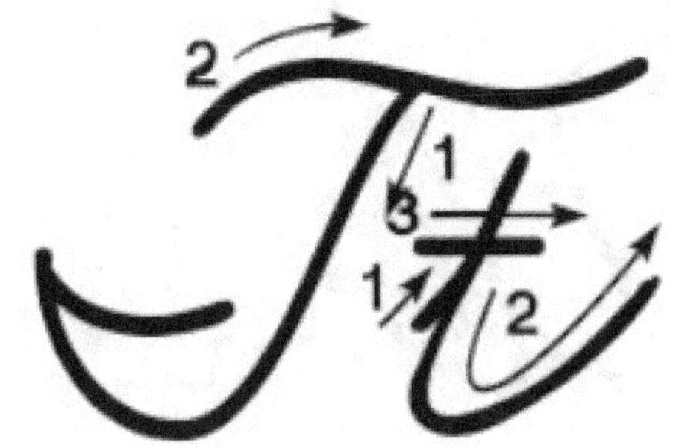

TRACE THEN WRITE ON YOUR OWN.

t   t   t   t   t

t   t   t   t

t

TRACE THEN WRITE ON YOUR OWN.

T   T   T   T

T   T   T

T

t

T

TRACE THEN WRITE ON YOUR OWN.

TRACE THEN WRITE ON YOUR OWN.

TRACE THEN WRITE ON YOUR OWN.

TRACE THEN WRITE ON YOUR OWN.

TRACE THEN WRITE ON YOUR OWN.

TRACE THEN WRITE ON YOUR OWN.

TRACE THEN WRITE ON YOUR OWN.

TRACE THEN WRITE ON YOUR OWN.

TRACE THEN WRITE ON YOUR OWN.

TRACE THEN WRITE ON YOUR OWN.

TRACE THEN WRITE ON YOUR OWN.

TRACE THEN WRITE ON YOUR OWN.

Lets practice words beginning with <u>uppercase</u>

Plate Plate Plate Plate

Something Something

Always Always Always

Teddy Teddy Teddy Teddy

Because Because Because

Cornfield   Cornfield

Pickles   Pickles   Pickles

Dalmatian   Dalmatian

Playground   Playground

Geologist   Geologist

Limestone   Limestone

Seagull   Seagull   Seagull

Hospital   Hospital   Hospital

Strawberry   Strawberry

Elephant   Elephant   Elephant

Volcano Volcano Volcano

Scientist Scientist Scientist

Experience   Experience

Become   Become   Become

Balloon Balloon Balloon

Atmosphere   Atmosphere

Dinosaur   Dinosaur

Chicken   Chicken   Chicken

Octopus   Octopus   Octopus

Bathroom   Bathroom

Instrument   Instrument

Toothpaste   Toothpaste

Vocabulary   Vocabulary

Pumpkin   Pumpkin

Underwear   Underwear

Honeycomb   Honeycomb
Pumpkin   Pumpkin
Ladder   Ladder   Ladder
Vacation Vacation Vacation
Noodles   Noodles   Noodles

Favorite   Favorite   Favorite

Tomato   Tomato   Tomato

Between   Between   Between

Anyone   Anyone   Anyone

Centipede   Centipede

Parrot   Parrot   Parrot

Afraid   Afraid   Afraid

Cabbage   Cabbage   Cabbage

Barrier   Barrier   Barrier

Haircut   Haircut   Haircut

Doorknob   Doorknob

Butter   Butter   Butter

Breakfast   Breakfast

Concentrate   Concentrate

Porcupines   Porcupines

Doorknob   Doorknob

Butter   Butter   Butter

Breakfast   Breakfast

Concentrate   Concentrate

Porcupines   Porcupines

Lets practice words

beginning

with <u>lowercase</u>

moonbeams	moonbeams

already	already	already

dishwasher	dishwasher

toothache	toothache

cupcake	cupcake

treatment   treatment

skeleton   skeleton   skeleton

impressive   impressive

nobody   nobody   nobody

cucumber   cucumber

between between between

birthday birthday birthday

toothless toothless toothless

battle battle battle

holiday holiday holiday

mushroom   mushroom

spaceman   spaceman

computer   computer

battle   battle   battle

billboards   billboards

mermaids   mermaids

entertainment

calendar   calendar   calendar

weather   weather   weather

soccer   soccer   soccer

kangaroo   kangaroo

yesterday   yesterday

building   building   building

promotion   promotion

exhibition   exhibition

restaurant restaurant

spaceman spaceman

sandpaper sandpaper

everyone everyone

everything everything

transparent transparent

invention invention

telephone telephone

pointless pointless

playground playground

sunglasses   sunglasses

student   student   student

snowman   snowman

celebrity   celebrity   celebrity

conditioner   conditioner

Read. Trace.
Make your own.

JOKES
FOR KIDS

Fun Cursive with Jokes, Riddles and Knock-knock!

It took 10 workers 10 days to build a bridge. How long would it take 5 workers to build the same bridge? None—it's already built!

LETS TRACE.

It took 10 workers 10 days to build a bridge. How long would it take 5 workers to build the same bridge? None—it's already built!

PRACTICE YOUR OWN.

Name: ______________________________

When you look for something, why is it always
in the last place you look?
Because when you find it, you stop looking.

LETS TRACE.

When you look for something, why is
it always in the last place you look?
Because when you find it, you stop
looking.

PRACTICE YOUR OWN.

Name: ________________________________

Two pickles fell out of a jar onto the floor. What did one say to the other?
Dill with it.

LETS TRACE.

Two pickles fell out of a jar onto the
floor.
What did one say to the other?
Dill with it.

PRACTICE YOUR OWN.

Name: ___________________________

What did the limestone say to the geologist?
Don't take me for granite!

LETS TRACE.

What did the limestone say to the geologist?
Don't take me for granite!

PRACTICE YOUR OWN.

Name: ________________________________

Fun Cursive with <u>Jokes</u>, Riddles and Knock-knock! 

Why does a seagull fly over the sea?
Because if it flew over the bay, it would be a
bay gull.

<u>LETS TRACE.</u>

<u>Why does a seagull fly over the sea?</u>

Because if it flew over the bay, it would

be a bay gull.

<u>PRACTICE YOUR OWN.</u>

Name: ______________________________

What do you think of that new diner on the moon?
Food was good, but there really wasn't much
atmosphere.

LETS TRACE.

What do you think of that new diner
on the moon?

Food was good, but there really wasn't
much atmosphere.

PRACTICE YOUR OWN.

Name: ______________________________

Kid: What are you doing under there?

Mom: Under where?

Kid: Ha ha! You said underwear!!

LETS TRACE.

Kid: What are you doing under there?

Mom: Under where?

Kid: Ha ha! You said underwear!!

PRACTICE YOUR OWN.

Name: _______________________

Why did Johnny throw the clock out of the window?
Because he wanted to see time fly.

LETS TRACE.

Why did Johnny throw the clock out of the window?
Because he wanted to see time fly.

PRACTICE YOUR OWN.

Name: ______________________________

Fun Cursive with Jokes, Riddles and Knock-knock!

What do you get when you cross an elephant with a fish?
Swimming trunks.

LETS TRACE.

What do you get when you cross an elephant with a fish?
Swimming trunks.

PRACTICE YOUR OWN.

Name: _______________________________

What's the difference between roast beef and pea soup?
Anyone can roast beef.

LETS TRACE.

What's the difference between roast
beef and pea soup?
Anyone can roast beef.

PRACTICE YOUR OWN.

Name: ________________________________

What do you get when you cross a centipede with a parrot?
A walkie talkie.

LETS TRACE.

What do you get when you cross a centipede with a parrot?
A walkie talkie.

PRACTICE YOUR OWN.

Name: ________________________________

> What sound do you hear when a cow breaks the
> sound barrier?
> Cowboom!

LETS TRACE.

What sound do you hear when a cow
breaks the sound barrier?
Cowboom!

PRACTICE YOUR OWN.

Name: ________________________________

What do you do if you get peanut butter on your doorknob?

Use a door jam.

LETS TRACE.

What do you do if you get peanut butter on your doorknob?

Use a door jam.

PRACTICE YOUR OWN.

Name: _______________________

Why did the teacher wear sunglasses to school?
Because her students were so bright.

LETS TRACE.

Why did the teacher wear sunglasses
to school?

Because her students were so bright.

PRACTICE YOUR OWN.

Name: _______________________________

RIDDLES FOR KIDS

Fun Cursive with Jokes, _Riddles_ and Knock-knock! 

Imagine you're in a room that is filling with water. There are no windows or doors. How do you get out?
A: Stop imagining!

LETS TRACE.

Imagine you're in a room that is filling with water. There are no windows or doors. How do you get out? A: Stop imagining!

PRACTICE YOUR OWN.

Name: _______________________________________

If you throw a blue stone into the Red Sea, what will it become?
A: Wet.

LETS TRACE.

If you throw a blue stone into the

Red Sea,

what will it become?

A: Wet.

PRACTICE YOUR OWN.

Name: ______________________________

What superhero is terrible at their job because they always get lost and are late?
A: "Wander" Woman.

LETS TRACE.

What superhero is terrible at their job because they always get lost and are late?
A: "Wander" Woman

PRACTICE YOUR OWN.

Name: ________________________________

What starts with a P, ends with an E and has thousands of letters?

A: Post office.

LETS TRACE.

What starts with a P, ends with an E and has thousands of letters?

A: Post office.

PRACTICE YOUR OWN.

Name: ______________________________

Fun Cursive with Jokes, _Riddles_ and Knock-knock!

You draw a line. Without touching it, how do you make the line longer?

A: You draw a shorter line next to it, and it becomes the longer line.

LETS TRACE.

You draw a line. Without touching it, how do you make the line longer?

A: You draw a shorter line next to it, and it becomes the longer line.

PRACTICE YOUR OWN.

Name: _______________________________

What goes around and around the wood, but never goes into the wood?

A: The bark on a tree.

LETS TRACE.

What goes around and around the

wood, but never goes into the wood?

A: The bark on a tree.

PRACTICE YOUR OWN.

Name: _______________________________

> *I give milk and I have a horn, but I'm not a cow. What am I?*
>
> *A: A milk truck.*

LETS TRACE.

I give milk and I have a horn, but

I'm not a cow. What am I?

A: A milk truck.

PRACTICE YOUR OWN.

Name: _______________________

Fun Cursive with Jokes, _Riddles_ and Knock-knock!

What is as light as a feather, but even the world's strongest man couldn't hold it for more than a minute?
A: His breath.

LETS TRACE.

What is as light as a feather, but even the world's strongest man couldn't hold it for more than a minute?
A: His breath

PRACTICE YOUR OWN.

Name: _______________________________

Fun Cursive with Jokes, _Riddles_ and Knock-knock! 

What belongs to you but other people use it more than you?
A: Your name.

LETS TRACE.

What belongs to you but other people use it more than you?
A: Your name.

PRACTICE YOUR OWN.

Name: ______________________

Which weighs more, a pound of feathers or a pound of bricks?

A: Neither. They both weigh one pound.

LETS TRACE.

Which weighs more, a pound of

feathers or a pound of bricks?

A: Neither. They both weigh one pound.

PRACTICE YOUR OWN.

Name: _______________________________

Using only addition, how do you add eight 8s and get the number 1,000?

A: 888 + 88 + 8 + 8 + 8 = 1000.

LETS TRACE.

Using only addition, how do you add eight 8s and get the number 1,000?

A: 888 + 88 + 8 + 8 + 8 = 1000.

PRACTICE YOUR OWN.

Name: ___________________________

You walk into a room with a match, a kerosene lamp, a candle, and a fireplace. Which do you light first?
A: The match.

LETS TRACE.

You walk into a room with a match, a kerosene lamp, a candle, and a fireplace. Which do you light first?
A: The match.

PRACTICE YOUR OWN.

Name: _______________________

> *Railroad crossing, watch out for cars. Can you spell that without any Rs?*
> *A: T-H-A-T.*

LETS TRACE.

Railroad crossing, watch out for cars.

Can you spell that without any Rs?

A: T-H-A-T.

PRACTICE YOUR OWN.

Name: ___________________________

Name four days of the week that start with the letter "T."
A: Tuesday, Thursday, today, and tomorrow.

<u>LETS TRACE.</u>

<u>Name four days of the week that start</u>

<u>with the letter "T."</u>

A: Tuesday, Thursday, today, and

tomorrow.

<u>PRACTICE YOUR OWN.</u>

Name: ________________________

A boy fell off a 20-foot ladder but did not get hurt. Why not?

A: He fell off the bottom step.

LETS TRACE.

A boy fell off a 20-foot ladder but did not get hurt. Why not?

A: He fell off the bottom step.

PRACTICE YOUR OWN.

Name: ________________________________

KNOCK-KNOCK JOKES

Knock, knock! Who's there?
Mikey! Mikey who?
Mikey doesn't fit in the hole!

LETS TRACE.

Knock, knock! Who's there?

Mikey! Mikey who?

Mikey doesn't fit in the hole!

PRACTICE YOUR OWN.

Name: ___________________________

Knock, knock!! Who's there?
A tish A tish who?
Bless you.

LETS TRACE.

Knock, knock!! Who's there?

A tish... A tish who?

Bless you.

PRACTICE YOUR OWN.

Name: _______________________

Fun Cursive with Jokes, Riddles and <u>Knock-knock!</u>

> Knock, knock! Who's there?
> Jamaican... Jamaican who?
> Jamaican me crazy!

LETS TRACE.

Knock, knock! Who's there?

Jamaican... Jamaican who?

Jamaican me crazy!

PRACTICE YOUR OWN.

Name: ________________________________

Fun Cursive with Jokes, Riddles and Knock-knock!

Knock knock!! Who's there?
Leaf? Leaf who?
Leaf me alone!

LETS TRACE.

Knock knock!! Who's there?

Leaf? Leaf who?

Leaf me alone!

PRACTICE YOUR OWN.

Name: ________________________________

Knock, knock!! Who's there?
Gorilla...Gorilla who?
Gorilla me a hamburger!

LETS TRACE.

Knock, knock!! Who's there?

Gorilla...Gorilla who?

Gorilla me a hamburger!

PRACTICE YOUR OWN.

Name: _______________________

Fun Cursive with Jokes, Riddles and Knock-knock! 

Knock, knock!! Who's there?

Noah...Noah who?

Noah good place to eat?

LETS TRACE.

Knock, knock!! Who's there?

Noah...Noah who?

Noah good place to eat?

PRACTICE YOUR OWN.

Name: ___________________________

Fun Cursive with Jokes, Riddles and <u>Knock-knock!</u> 

> *Knock, knock!! Who's there?*
> *Your mom...   Your mom who?*
> *Your mom! Now open the door or you're grounded.*

LETS TRACE.

Knock, knock!! Who's there?

Your mom...   Your mom who?

Your mom! Now open the door or

you're grounded.

PRACTICE YOUR OWN.

Name: ______________________________

Fun Cursive with Jokes, Riddles and <u>Knock-knock!</u> 

Knock Knock!!   Who's there?
Tarzan! Tarzan who?
Tarzan stripes forever.

<u>LETS TRACE.</u>

Knock Knock!!   Who's there?

Tarzan! Tarzan who?

Tarzan stripes forever.

<u>PRACTICE YOUR OWN.</u>

Name: _______________________________

Fun Cursive with Jokes, Riddles and <u>Knock-knock!</u>

Knock, knock!!   Who's there?
Tennessee...   Tennessee who?
Tennessee is played at Wimbledon!

LETS TRACE.

Knock, knock!!   Who's there?

Tennessee...   Tennessee who?

Tennessee is played at Wimbledon!

PRACTICE YOUR OWN.

Name: ____________________

Fun Cursive with Jokes, Riddles and <u>Knock-knock!</u> 

Knock, knock!! Who's there?
You...   You who?
I didn't know you were so happy to meet me!

LETS TRACE.

Knock, knock!! Who's there?

You...   You who?

I didn't know you were so happy to

meet me!

PRACTICE YOUR OWN.

Name: ___________________________

Fun Cursive with Jokes, Riddles and <u>Knock-knock!</u>

Knock, knock!!   Who's there?
Water...   Water who?
Water you doing in my house!?

<u>LETS TRACE.</u>

Knock, knock!!   Who's there?

Water...   Water who?

Water you doing in my house!?

<u>PRACTICE YOUR OWN.</u>

Name: _______________________

Knock, knock!!   Who's there?
Nun...   Nun who?
Nun of your business!

LETS TRACE.

Knock, knock!!   Who's there?

Nun...   Nun who?

Nun of your business!

PRACTICE YOUR OWN.

Name: _______________________________

Fun Cursive with Jokes, Riddles and <u>Knock-knock!</u>

> Knock, knock!! Who's there?
> Justin... Justin who?
> Just in time for school!

LETS TRACE.

Knock, knock!! Who's there?

Justin... Justin who?

Just in time for school!

PRACTICE YOUR OWN.

Name: ______________________________

Fun Cursive with Jokes, Riddles and <u>Knock-knock!</u>

Knock, knock!!!   Who's there?
Amish...   Amish who?
Awe, I miss you too.

LETS TRACE.

Knock, knock!!!   Who's there?

Amish...   Amish who?

Awe, I miss you too.

PRACTICE YOUR OWN.

Name: _______________________________

Knock, knock!!! Who's there?
Dishes... Dishes who?
Dishes your friend!

LETS TRACE.

Knock, knock!!! Who's there?

Dishes... Dishes who?

Dishes your friend!

PRACTICE YOUR OWN.

Name: _______________________